TIMELINE *of the*
RENAISSANCE

By Charlie Samuels

Gareth Stevens
Publishing

Please visit our Web site www.garethstevens.com. For a free color catalog of all our high-quality books, call toll free 1-800-542-2595 or fax 1-877-542-2596.

Library of Congress Cataloging-in-Publication Data
Samuels, Charlie, 1961-
    Timeline of the Renaissance / Charlie Samuels.
      p. cm. — (History highlights)
    Includes index.
    ISBN 978-1-4339-3486-5 (library binding)
    ISBN 978-1-4339-3487-2 (pbk.)
    ISBN 978-1-4339-3488-9 (6-pack)
    1. Renaissance—Chronology—Juvenile literature. I. Title.
  CB361.S36 2010
  940.2'1—dc22   2009041582

Published in 2010 by
Gareth Stevens Publishing
111 East 14th Street, Suite 349
New York, NY 10003

© 2010 The Brown Reference Group Ltd.

For Gareth Stevens Publishing:
Art Direction: Haley Harasymiw
Editorial Direction: Kerri O'Donnell

For The Brown Reference Group Ltd:
Editorial Director: Lindsey Lowe
Managing Editor: Tim Cooke
Editor: Ben Hollingum
Children's Publisher: Anne O'Daly
Design Manager: David Poole
Designer: Karen Perry
Picture Manager: Sophie Mortimer
Production Director: Alastair Gourlay

Picture Credits:
Front Cover: Corbis: The Gallery Collection:

Corbis: Bettmann 41t; Olivier Martel: 39t; istockphoto: Duncan: 16; Nikada: 33b; Jupiter Images: Photos.com: 7, 12 inset, 17t, 18, 19, 20, 21t, 22-23, 23, 25t, 26-27, 29t, 30, 32, 33t, 35, 37. 39b. 42. 43, 45; Stockxpert: 5, 9t, 10, 11b, 13, 14, 15, 17b, 21b, 24, 25b, 26b, 28, 29b, 31, 34, 38, 41b, 44; Shutterstock: Kenneth V. Pilon: 6, 8; Dariusz Sas: 9b

All Artworks Brown Reference Group

Publisher's note to educators and parents: Our editors have carefully reviewed the Web sites that appear on p. 47 to ensure that they are suitable for students. Many Web sites change frequently, however, and we cannot guarantee that a site's future contents will continue to meet our high standards of quality and educational value. Be advised that students should be closely supervised whenever they access the Internet.

Manufactured in the United States of America
1 2 3 4 5 6 7 8 9 12 11 10

CPSIA compliance information: Batch #BRW0102GS: For further information contact Gareth Stevens, New York, New York at 1-800-542-2595.

Contents

Introduction 4

The Spread of Printing 6

The Age of Discovery 10

Guns and Gunpowder 16

The Renaissance 20

Leonardo da Vinci 24

Copernicus and the Universe 28

The Reformation 32

Ivan the Terrible 38

Elizabeth's England 42

Glossary 46

Further Reading 47

Index 48

Introduction

The Renaissance is the name given to a period in European history that lasted from roughly 1375 to 1575. It was a time of great discovery and change in the world.

Mariners from Europe found the Americas and new sea routes to the Spice Islands of Asia. Gold and silver from the New World and the increase in trade made some Europeans extremely rich. They spent their wealth on luxury goods like paintings for their homes, and this created a new demand for the work of artists of all kinds. Europe experienced a cultural flowering as great painters like Leonardo da Vinci, Michelangelo, and Raphael produced masterpieces that are still admired today. Meanwhile, European scholars rediscovered the works of ancient Greek and Roman writers. This led to a new way of looking at the world based on observation and the importance of the individual. This humanism, together with other new ideas, spread more rapidly than ever before thanks to the introduction of printing with movable type.

Religious Change

There was upheaval in the church, too. Thinkers such as Erasmus and Luther began to question the teachings of the established church. This eventually led to a breakaway from the Catholic Church and the setting up of Protestant churches —an event called the Reformation.

About This Book

This book focuses on the 200 years from 1400 to 1600 in Europe, where the Renaissance occurred. It contains two different types of timelines. Along the bottom of the pages is a timeline that covers the whole period. It lists key events and developments, color-coded by region. Each chapter also has its own timeline, running vertically down the sides of the pages. This timeline provides more details about the particular subject of the chapter.

The city of Florence in Tuscany was one of the centers of the Italian Renaissance. ⬇

The Spread of Printing

The printing press revolutionized fifteenth-century Europe. Now books could be produced cheaply, allowing a wider circulation—and spreading new ideas.

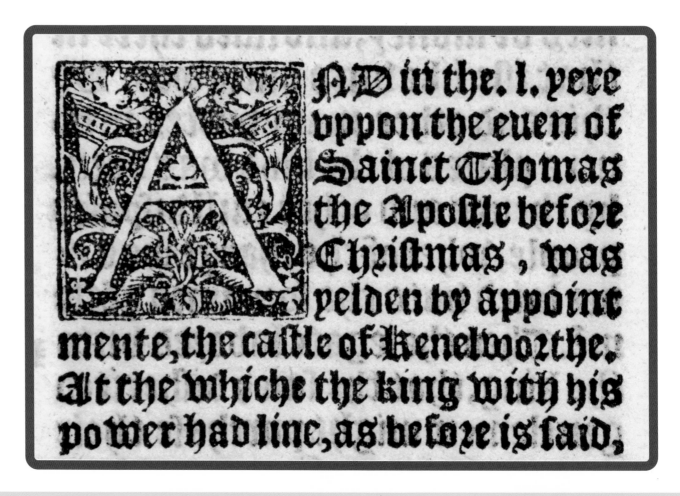

TIMELINE
1400–1410

c.1400 The lost-wax method of bronze-casting is used in West Africa.

1401 The Mongol leader Timur sacks Baghdad in Iraq.

1404 Death of Harihara, ruler of the Hindu kingdom of Vijaynagar in southern India.

1400

1402

1404

KEY:

EUROPE

ASIA

AFRICA

c.1400 The French historian Jean Froissart writes a record of the Hundred Years' War.

1402 Timur defeats and captures the Ottoman sultan Bayezid in Anatolia.

c.1403 Lorenzo Ghiberti designs the bronze doors of the Baptistery in Florence.

The person credited with setting up Europe's first printing press was a German, Johannes Gutenberg. The first book he printed, in about 1455, was the Bible. Gutenberg did not invent printing, however. The Chinese were printing books at least as early as the eighth century. They carved a text onto a block of wood so that the characters stood out in relief, spread ink on the block, laid a sheet of paper on it, and transferred the inked text by rubbing the back of the paper. Europeans were using similar methods to print religious pictures and short texts by the early fifteenth century.

← Early printed books sometimes had ornate initial letters, like old manuscripts.

Timeline of Printing

c.750 By this time the Chinese are employing woodblocks to print single-sheet publications.

c.900 Woodblock printing is widely employed by this date in China, Japan, and Korea.

1399 Johannes Gutenberg is born in Mainz, Germany; he later works as a silversmith.

c.1420 Woodcuts are printed in Germany.

c.1430 Printing with engraved metal plates is used in Holland and Germany.

c. 1435 Laurens Janszoon Koster experiments with movable type in Haarlem; some claim he invented it before Gutenberg.

← Johannes Gutenberg trained as a silversmith before becoming a printer.

1407 Shah Rokh becomes sole ruler of the Timurid Empire in Iran and central Asia.

1410 A Polish-Lithuanian army defeats the Teutonic knights at the Battle of Tannenberg and begins the Jagiellon Dynasty of Polish kings.

1406

1408

1410

1405 The Chinese emperor Yongle sponsors the first ocean exploration by Admiral Zheng He.

c.1410 Most of the stone buildings in Great Zimbabwe have now been built.

Timeline (continued)

1438 Gutenberg begins experimenting with printing at Strasbourg.

c.1455 Gutenberg publishes the first commercially printed book, the Gutenberg Bible, at Mainz, Germany.

1457 Color printing is first used in the Mainz Psalter.

1468 Nicolaus Jensen establishes a printing shop in Venice; he experiments with different typefaces.

1476 William Caxton sets up a printing press in London, England.

1498 The first book of music is printed using movable type.

The Nuremberg Chronicle, a world history published in 1493, was illustrated with woodcuts.

Movable Type

Gutenberg's innovation was to develop a way of printing using reusable movable type. These rectangular pieces of cast metal, each bearing a raised letter, were arranged on a strip of wood to form words and sentences. They could then be taken apart and reset to print something else. Again, the Chinese had invented movable type long before, but because Chinese script has up to 60,000 different characters, the technology was not practical. Printing in European languages required only pieces of type for the letters of the alphabet, numerals, and punctuation marks, a much easier undertaking.

The printer placed the lines of type within a frame known as a form. After use, the type was removed from the form, broken up, and stored in a case to be used again. To print a page, the inked form was covered with

TIMELINE 1410–1420

1412 The last Tughluq sultan of Delhi, Nasiruddin Muhammad, dies.

1414 The Sayyid dynasty takes over the Delhi sultanate.

1414 The powerful Medici family of Florence become bankers to the pope.

1410   1412   1414

KEY:

EUROPE

ASIA

AFRICA

1410 Black Sheep Turkmen establish a dynasty in Baghdad.

c.1413 The Flemish Limbourg Brothers paint a Book of Hours (a collection of prayers) for the Duke of Berry; it is one of the most beautiful books of the Renaissance.

1414 A great council of the Catholic Church is held at Constance in Germany.

⋏ The printing press copied presses used to crush grapes.

a sheet of paper and placed between two wooden boards in the press. The printer turned a screw to press the upper surface (the *platen*) down onto the sheet of paper. Such presses had been in use since Roman times for pressing grapes and were used for binding manuscript books.

Gutenberg's press soon had many imitators. There was a market for books among the growing numbers of literate people—lawyers, merchants, teachers, and skilled artisans—in Europe's expanding cities. As presses were set up in city after city, a stream of bibles, encyclopedias, religious works, classics, histories, and romances poured out to feed the demand for the printed word.

Movable type comprised pieces of metal with raised letters that could be arranged into words. ⇒

Early Books

Books printed before 1501 are known as incunabula. The word comes from the Latin for "cradle." Early printers tried to copy the look of manuscripts. They used decorative typefaces or left space for initial letters to be decorated by hand. The books were large—people sat at tables to read. Usually only 200 or 300 copies of a book were printed at a time. Today some 35,000 incunabula survive.

1415 The Council of Constance condemns the Czech religious reformer Jan Hus to death.

1416 A Chinese fleet led by Admiral Zheng He sails on a great journey of exploration to east Africa.

1419 Prince Henry (the Navigator) of Portugal retires from royal duties to study navigation and seamanship.

1416

1418

1420

1415 King Henry V of England invades France; he wins a great victory at the Battle of Agincourt.

1417 The Council of Constance elects Martin V as pope, ending the division, or schism, in the Catholic Church.

1420 Henry V of England marries his daughter Catherine to the French king, who in return makes Henry his heir.

The Age of Discovery

European sailors traditionally avoided the open Atlantic Ocean. Although the Vikings had reached Newfoundland around the year 1000, their feat had long been forgotten.

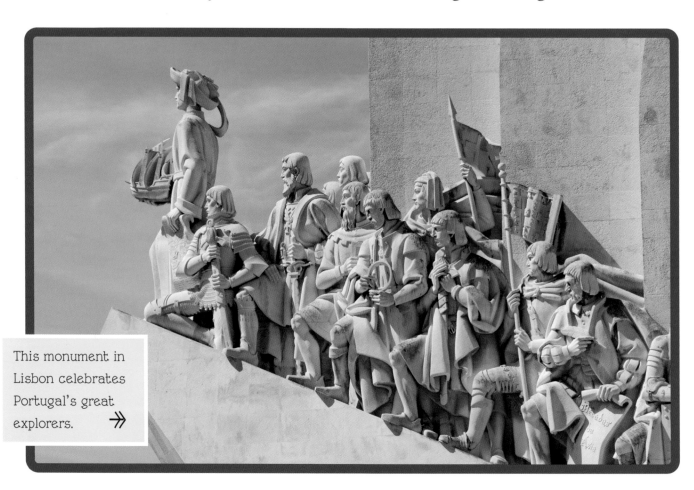

This monument in Lisbon celebrates Portugal's great explorers. →

TIMELINE
1420–1430

1420 The Italian architect Filippo Brunelleschi begins to build the dome of Florence Cathedral in Italy; the marvel of engineering takes until 1461 to complete.

c.1425 In the Americas, the farming Hohokam Culture dies out, probably as a result of crop failure.

1420   1422   1424

KEY:

EUROPE

ASIA

AFRICA, AMERICAS

1420 In Bohemia (now the Czech Republic), supporters of Jan Hus reject the authority of the Holy Roman Emperor and begin a 13-year war.

1421 The Forbidden City is completed in Beijing, China, which becomes the permanent imperial capital.

In the Middle Ages, trading boats rarely ventured far from the sight of land. By the end of the fifteenth century, however, Portuguese ships had voyaged far into the Atlantic and sailed around Africa into the Indian Ocean, while Christopher Columbus had reached the Americas. The Age of Discovery had begun.

Navigation depended on instruments such as this astrolabe, which calculated the position of the sun. ⇓

Trade Routes

The most pressing reason why European sailors began to venture into the Atlantic was trade. Muslim states had won control of the western end of the overland routes from China and India, along which luxury goods such as silk, spices, gold, and rubies traveled to Europe. Some individuals therefore began to seek alternative routes to these riches.

On the edge of Europe, the Portuguese knew that supplies of gold and slaves reached the Muslim cities of

Timeline of the Age of Discovery

1420 The Portuguese discover the Madeira Islands, west of Morocco.

1432 The Portuguese colonize the Atlantic islands called the Azores.

1434 Portuguese navigator Gil Eanes passes Cape Bojador on the Moroccan coast.

1445 The Portuguese round Cape Verde, the westernmost tip of Africa.

1480 The astrolabe (for measuring latitude from the height of the sun) is adapted for use at sea.

1488 Bartholomeu Dias rounds the Cape of Good Hope, the southern tip of Africa.

⇐ The Cape of Good Hope marks the southern tip of Africa. Dias sailed around it in 1488.

1429 After Joan of Arc leads a French army to recapture Orléans, the Dauphin is crowned King Charles VII of France, a turning point in the Hundred Years' War.

1426

1428

1430

1426 Mamelukes from Syria and Egypt raid Cyprus.

c.1430 East African traders introduce coffee to Arabia.

Timeline (continued)

1492 Christopher Columbus makes his first voyage to the Americas, visiting Hispaniola and Cuba.

1497 Vasco da Gama sails from Lisbon to Calicut, on the west coast of India.

1497 Italian John Cabot sails to Canada on behalf of English king Henry VII.

1498 On his third voyage, Columbus reaches mainland South America.

1500 The Portuguese navigator Pedro Cabral discovers the coast of Brazil.

➡ Exploration made the countries of the Atlantic seaboard Europe's economic focus.

A sketch shows da Gama's ships on the way to India. ➡

North Africa by overland routes across the Sahara from the south. In the early 1400s, they began to venture south by sea down the African coast, and by the 1440s, they had reached west Africa. The prevailing north winds in that part of the Atlantic made the return journey to Portugal hazardous, but the sea

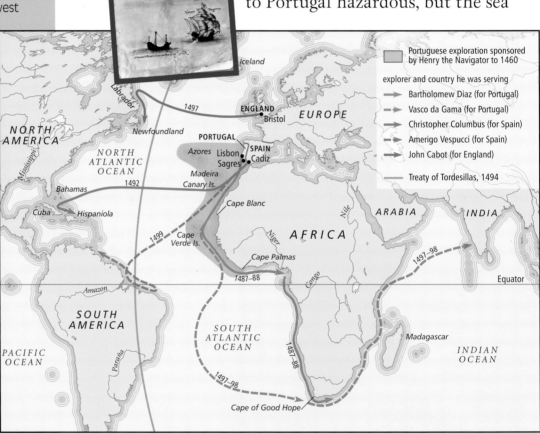

TIMELINE
1430–1440

1434 Portuguese navigator Gil Eanes sails around the coast of Morocco, opening the way for European exploration of the coast of west Africa.

1434 Cosimo de Medici makes the Medici the effective rulers of Florence, Italy.

1430   1432   1434

1430 Joan of Arc is captured and handed to the English, who execute her as a witch.

1434 The Sayyid sultan of Delhi, Mubarak Shah, is assassinated.

KEY:

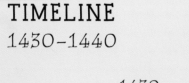

EUROPE

ASIA

AFRICA, AMERICAS

captains discovered that by sailing far out into the Atlantic, they could find southerly winds that would bring them safely home. Soon the Portuguese were sending regular shipments of gold and slaves back to Lisbon each year from the fortified trading stations they set up along the African coast.

In 1488, Bartholomeu Dias sailed around the southernmost tip of Africa and into the Indian Ocean, and a decade later, Vasco da Gama became the first westerner to reach India by the sea route around the coast of Africa. He had opened up a direct passage to the wealth of Asia.

To the New World

Meanwhile, Christopher Columbus, in the service of King Ferdinand and Queen Isabella of Spain, had sailed west across the Atlantic in search of a sea route to China and came upon the Americas instead. Italian by birth,

Prince Henry was partly inspired by a ⟫ wish to drive Muslims from North Africa.

Henry the Navigator

The guiding spirit behind Portugal's exploration was Prince Henry the Navigator. Henry was a Christian who wanted to drive the Muslims out of North Africa. Henry aimed to contact Prester John, a legendary Christian ruler in Africa. He thought that by sailing down the coast of Africa, a fleet might meet up with the king's forces to launch a combined crusade against the Muslims of Morocco.

1436 At the Council of Basel, the Catholic Church agrees to readmit most of the Hussites, religious reformers from Bohemia (now the Czech Republic).

1438 The Mongol khanate of the Golden Horde breaks up into a number of smaller khanates, including Crimea and Astrakhan.

1436   1438   1440

1437 A Portuguese expedition to capture Tangiers in North Africa, led by Prince Henry, fails badly.

1438 Albert of Hapsburg is elected Holy Roman Emperor; from now on, the title becomes the hereditary possession of the Hapsburg family.

1439 Jahan Shah becomes leader of the Black Sheep Turkmen; he is known as a patron of the arts.

Practical Advances

At his court at Sagres, on the southwest tip of Portugal, Henry the Navigator brought together mapmakers and astronomers. His shipbuilders developed the caravel, a deep-bottomed boat that could turn quickly in the wind and was sturdy enough for long sea voyages. By the time of Henry's death, Portuguese caravels had sailed as far as Sierra Leone in west Africa.

Caravels, like this reconstruction, were broad and squat. →

Columbus had spent many years as a sea captain in Lisbon, sailing as far north as Iceland and south to Sierra Leone. He studied the accounts of the Venetian traveler Marco Polo's journeys in Asia and pored over maps and works of astronomy. Based on his studies, he calculated that the island Polo called Cipangu (Japan) lay only about 2,000 miles (3,200 km) to the west of Europe.

A Remarkable Voyage

This was a serious underestimate, as Japan is actually about 12,000 miles (19,000 km) distant. But Columbus's error does not detract from his skill as a navigator in guiding his three tiny vessels across the Atlantic Ocean. Facing the threat of mutiny from his crew, Columbus continued westward on his voyage to make landfall in the Bahamas on October 12, 1492. He returned to the Americas three more times in the service of Spain.

TIMELINE
1440–1450

KEY:

Europe

Asia

Africa, Americas

1443 A Persian visiting Vijayanagar in southern India declares the city to have "no equal in the world."

1443 At the Battle of Zlatica, Ottomans defeat Hungarian resistance to their advance in the Balkans.

1440

1442

1444

1441 Portuguese traders export the first slaves from Africa to Europe.

1443 King Alfonso of Aragon and Sicily also becomes king of Naples.

1444 A Crusade against the Ottomans led by the papacy is easily defeated at Varna on the Black Sea.

Christopher Columbus

Christopher Columbus is one of the most controversial figures of the Age of Discovery. Critics say that his "discovery" of the Americas was a disaster for the millions of people who already lived there. The Europeans brought diseases that wiped out whole settlements. Other native people died in wars. The survivors were often enslaved to work for the newcomers on farms or in mines. In the end, native groups either died out or lost their land.

The compass was used in Europe from the twelfth century.

Supporters of Columbus say that it is wrong to hold him responsible for what happened after his voyages. At the time, no one knew how diseases spread, for example. There was no way Columbus could have known that native peoples would have no resistance to European sicknesses.

Columbus, however, is still recognized as the man who brought together the Old and New Worlds. His voyages changed history—for better or worse.

Columbus points west across the Atlantic in this statue in Barcelona. The Spanish port was where his first voyage finished.

c.1450 The Shona on the Zambezi River control the gold trade in southeastern Africa.

1446   1448   1450

1445 The Dominican monk and artist Fra Angelico paints a series of frescoes in Rome.

c.1450 The Syrian cities of Aleppo and Damascus control the textile trade between Europe and Asia.

Guns and Gunpowder

Gunpowder was invented in China in the eleventh century; it spread to Europe 300 years later. Gunpowder and the firearms that used it changed history.

⇐ Crusaders use cannons to attack Tunis in North Africa in 1390.

TIMELINE
1450–1460

1452 Italian architect Leon Battista Alberti publishes *On Architecture*, a major influence on the classical revival during the Renaissance.

1453 The Hundred Years' War ends when the French drive the English from France.

1455 Construction of the Great Bazaar begins in Constantinople, now renamed Istanbul.

1450   1452   1454

KEY:

EUROPE

ASIA

AFRICA

c.1450 Johannes Gutenberg sets up a printing press in Mainz, Germany.

1453 The Byzantine Empire ends when the Ottoman Turks capture Constantinople.

1455 In England, the Tudor and Lancastrian families begin the Wars of the Roses to win the throne.

The origins of gunpowder are shrouded in mystery, mainly because the people who invented it wanted to keep it a secret. The first written mention comes from Chinese writer Tseng Kung Liang in 1044, who calls it the "fire drug."

Gunpowder is a mixture of charcoal, sulfur, and saltpeter (potassium nitrate). When mixed, it burns rapidly, producing hot gases. The gases expand and, if confined inside a container, explode with a loud bang. If burned at the closed end of an open-ended tube, the expanding gases will push out a ball or bullet. This is the principle behind the cannon and all firearms.

← Attackers besiege a castle in this print from the seventeenth century.

Timeline of Guns and Gunpowder

c.1020 Invention of gunpowder.

1044 The first written mention of gunpowder, in China.

1100 The first fireworks are invented in China, where they are hugely popular.

1220 The first gunpowder bombs are recorded.

1242 Roger Bacon writes a description of gunpowder.

1280 The gunpowder cannon is made from barrels linked together.

1375 Bronze cannons are successfully cast.

1540 A safe form of cast-iron cannon is created.

Castle walls grew thicker, taller, and stronger as cannons became more powerful. →

1456 Vlad becomes prince of Wallachia in southern Romania; his cruel execution of his enemies earns him the nickname "Vlad the Impaler."

1456   1458   1460

1458 Matthias I Corvinus is elected king of Hungary.

Small Arms

The first "small arm" was the *arquebus* or hackbut, invented in Spain in the 1400s. Within a century, it was replaced by the more effective musket. The musket was ignited by a flintlock, fired by sparks from a flint. The musket's smooth bore gave way to the rifle, which had a spiral-grooved barrel to spin the ball or bullet. The final development was the breech-loading rifle. Handguns followed a similar development from muzzle-loading flintlock pistols to cartridge weapons.

With the advent of gunpowder, fireworks became popular in China in the 1100s, usually in the form of strings of firecrackers. Gunpowder bombs were more dangerous. In about 1220, the Chinese made bombs that shattered on explosion, producing a kind of shrapnel to kill or wound the enemy. In 1226, Chinese soldiers used grenades and "fire arrows"—probably rockets—in the defense of Kaifeng. The knowledge spread abroad, and there is a reference to saltpeter and rockets in a 1280 Syrian book on warfare.

↑ A sixteenth-century Italian soldier carries a heavy arquebus over his shoulder.

← Gunners calculate the angle to fire their cannon at its target.

TIMELINE
1460–1470

1461 French poet François Villon writes his masterpiece, *Testament.*

1460

1462

1464

KEY:

EUROPE

ASIA

AFRICA

1463 Mahmud Gawan becomes chief minister of the Bahmani kingdom on India's Deccan Plateau.

Coming of the Cannon

The gunpowder cannon originated in the late 1280s, in the Chinese military. By about 1300, Arab technicians made cannon barrels from bamboo tubes bound around with iron bands. In 1346, the English used wrought-iron cannons, called bombards, against the French at the siege of Calais, and a year later, European gunsmiths made arrow-firing cannons. The first cannon barrels cast as a single piece in bronze can be dated to Germany in 1378. Cast iron could not be used for barrels at first because the castings were often flawed, causing disastrous explosions. The cast iron smashed into fragments, like a bomb. When a bronze cannon barrel failed it tore or ruptured, with less tragic results. French gunners used cast iron to make cannonballs from about 1495, and safe cast-iron barrels were first made in England in 1543.

Berthold Schwarz may have reinvented gunpowder independently or learned about it from travelers. →

Berthold Schwarz

Berthold Schwarz is often identified as the monk Konstantin Anklitzen, who lived in Freiburg, Germany, in about 1320. He was called Schwarz ("black") because of the smoke that surrounded his alchemical experiments. He is often given credit for the invention (or reinvention) of gunpowder. In fact, the ingredients of the explosive had already been written down by English scientist Roger Bacon (c.1214–92) in 1242.

1467 In Japan, the Onin War undermines the power of the shogun and leads to the rise of warlords called *daimyo*.

1469 Lorenzo "the Magnificent" Medici comes to power in Florence; he gathers many great artists to his court.

1466   1468   1470

1467 The White Sheep Turkmen of northern Iraq defeat the Black Sheep Turkmen and take their territory.

1468 Qa'itbay begins a 28-year reign as Mameluke sultan; he extensively restores the shrines of Mecca and Medina in Arabia.

The Renaissance

The word "renaissance" means rebirth. It refers to an artistic and cultural movement that arose in northern Italy in the 14th century and had spread throughout Europe by the mid-16th century.

Michelangelo painted the Sistine Chapel in Rome with scenes from the Bible. ⇒

TIMELINE
1470–1480

1472 Grand Prince Ivan of Moscow marries Zoe, the niece of the last Byzantine emperor.

1474 Isabella, wife of King Ferdinand I of Aragon, becomes queen of Castile; her inheritance unites the two most powerful Spanish kingdoms.

1470   1472   1474

KEY:

EUROPE

ASIA

AFRICA

1471 Death of the Dutch monk Thomas à Kempis, whose book *Imitation of Christ* is one of the most important medieval books about the Christian faith.

1472 Leonardo da Vinci quits the workshop of the artist Andrea del Verrochio and sets up as an independent artist.

1474 The Chinese repair the Great Wall to keep out Mongol raiders who live beyond it.

↑ The dome of the cathedral towers over the city of Florence.

In its origins, the Renaissance looked backward. It sought inspiration in the art and literature of the classical worlds of Greece and Rome. There had been revivals of interest in the classical past before. A new factor in the fourteenth and fifteenth centuries was the decline of the Byzantine Empire. Greek scholars took many classical manuscripts to Italy for safety. Previously unknown in the West, these works opened new branches of study in fields such as medicine, math, geography, and philosophy.

By the early fifteenth century, Italian cities such as Florence, Ferrara, Urbino, Venice, and Milan had become wealthy through trade and banking. They were creative centers where artists and craftsmen such as the architects

This *Pietà* by Michelangelo shows Mary holding Jesus' dead body. ➔

Timeline of the Renaissance

c.1420 The architect Brunelleschi, the sculptor Donatello, and the painter Masaccio work in Florence.

1434 Cosimo de Medici begins a 30-year domination of Florence.

1485 Sandro Botticelli paints the *Birth of Venus*.

1506 Leonardo da Vinci paints the *Mona Lisa*.

1508 Michelangelo begins to paint the ceiling of the Sistine Chapel.

1508 The painter Raphael is employed by Pope Julian II to decorate the papal chambers in the Vatican.

1509 Erasmus publishes *In Praise of Folly*.

1476 Spaniards settle in the Canary Islands off Africa.

1478 The Spanish church sets up the Inquisition, a religious court to enforce the Catholic faith.

1479 A 15-year war between Venice and the Ottoman Empire ends in a peace treaty.

1480 The Russians stop paying tribute to the Mongol rulers of the Khanate of the Golden Horde.

1476   1478   1480

1476 Charles the Bold of Burgundy fails to conquer the Swiss.

1477 The Hapsburgs, rulers of the Holy Roman Empire, acquire the Netherlands by marriage.

1478 In Florence, Italy, a feud between the Medici and Pazzi families for control of the city ends in a massacre of the Pazzis.

Timeline (continued)

1513 Niccolo Machiavelli publishes *The Prince*, a handbook for rulers.

1516 Sir Thomas More writes *Utopia*, in which he describes an ideal form of government.

1543 Nicolaus Copernicus sets the sun at the center of the universe.

1547 Michelangelo is made architect of St. Peter's in Rome.

c.1550 Giorgio Vasari publishes *The Lives of the Artists*— biographies of the great Renaissance painters.

Alberti and Brunelleschi and the painters Donatello and Masaccio were developing new styles of architecture and art based on the ideals of the past. Powerful families such as the Medici of Florence and the Sforza of Milan became great patrons of the arts. They built libraries and churches in the classical style and funded universities

major cultural center

Italy in the mid 16th century
- Genoese territory
- Papal States
- Spanish Habsburg lands
- Venetian territory
- other Italian states

SAVOY
MILAN
Milan
Pavia
Turin
Cremona
Parma
Genoa
Carpi
GENOA
Pisa
Nice
Ligurian Sea
Piombino
FLORENCE
Siena
SIENA
Ajaccio
Corsica
Rome

VICENZA
VENICE
Asolo
Verona
Vicenza
Mantua
Sabbioneta
Ferrara
Bologna
Venice
Padua
Pola
Trieste
Zara
Florence
Urbino
PAPAL STATES
Perugia
Viterbo
Adriatic Sea
Ragusa

KINGDOM OF NAPLES
Benevento
Naples
Salerno
Lecce

KINGDOM OF SARDINIA
Tyrrhenian Sea
Cagliari

Reggio
Palermo
KINGDOM OF SICILY
Catania
Ionian Sea
Tunis
Pantelleria

0   200 km
0   150 mi

« Renaissance Italy was a land of rival city-states that competed to employ the best artists and architects.

The Renaissance ideal city had order and proportion. ⇓

TIMELINE 1480–1490

1481 Bayezid II becomes Ottoman sultan; he will oversee an expansion of Ottoman power.

1480   1482   1484

KEY:

EUROPE

ASIA

AFRICA

1480 An Ottoman fleet raids the Greek island of Rhodes and Otranto in southern Italy.

1485 In England, the Battle of Bosworth Field ends the Wars of the Roses and brings the Tudors to the throne.

where scholars could work. Partly through the new medium of printing and partly as a result of wars that brought foreign rulers to Italy, the influence of the Renaissance traveled to all the courts of Europe.

Humanists and Humanism

The scholars of the New Learning, as it was called, found inspiration in the works of classical writers to challenge the authority of the medieval church. They were known as humanists, reflecting their people-centered view of the universe. In art, humanist influence called for a more realistic depiction of nature, as seen in the works of Leonardo da Vinci (1452–1519). As well as a painter and sculptor, he was an architect and engineer, and his notebooks reveal a fertile mind, far ahead of his time in the study of biology, anatomy, mechanics, and aerodynamics.

Erasmus of Rotterdam

Desiderius Erasmus (1466–1536) was the most famous scholar of the Renaissance. He embraced humanism's belief in the power of human reason. He worked at many universities, and wrote to Europe's leading scholars. He was one of the first popular writers of the age of printing—his book *In Praise of Folly* went into 43 editions in his lifetime.

« Erasmus was painted by leading portrait artist Hans Holbein.

1486 *Malleus Maleficarum* (The Hammer of Witches) is published by two German monks. It becomes a handbook for a witch-hunting craze throughout Europe.

1486   1488   1490

1486 Sandro Botticelli paints the *Birth of Venus*.

1488 Portuguese sailor Bartolomeu Dias becomes the first European to sail around the Cape of Good Hope, at the southern tip of Africa.

Leonardo da Vinci

Leonardo da Vinci was an Italian artist, architect, sculptor, and engineer, with one of the most versatile minds of all time.

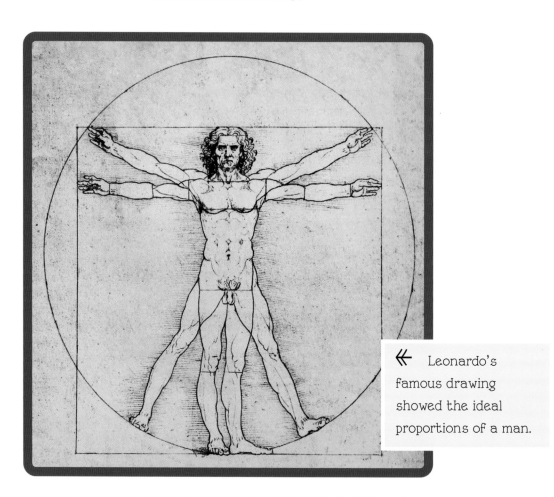

⇐ Leonardo's famous drawing showed the ideal proportions of a man.

TIMELINE
1490–1500

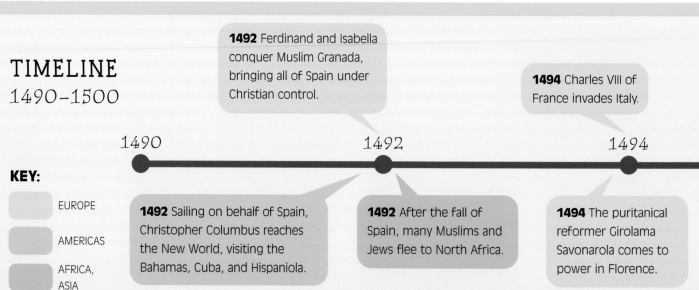

1492 Ferdinand and Isabella conquer Muslim Granada, bringing all of Spain under Christian control.

1494 Charles VIII of France invades Italy.

1490   1492   1494

KEY:

EUROPE

AMERICAS

AFRICA, ASIA

1492 Sailing on behalf of Spain, Christopher Columbus reaches the New World, visiting the Bahamas, Cuba, and Hispaniola.

1492 After the fall of Spain, many Muslims and Jews flee to North Africa.

1494 The puritanical reformer Girolama Savonarola comes to power in Florence.

Vinci is a small town near Florence in Italy. Leonardo was born there in 1452, the illegitimate son of a lawyer known as Ser Piero da Vinci. He was brought up by Piero's family and, at the age of 16, became an apprentice to painter and sculptor Andrea del Verrochio (1435–88). In 1482, Leonardo moved to Milan to work for Ludovico Sforza (1452–1508), later duke of Milan. While there, he painted the *Virgin of the Rocks* as part of the altarpiece of a chapel in Milan. In 1497, he created the mural *The Last Supper* at the monastery of Santa Maria delle Grazie. Driven from Milan by the French army in 1499, Leonardo returned to Florence. Three years later, he entered the service of Cesare Borgia

⬆ Leonardo was one of the most versatile men of his time. His paintings, drawings, and notes show a wide range of skills.

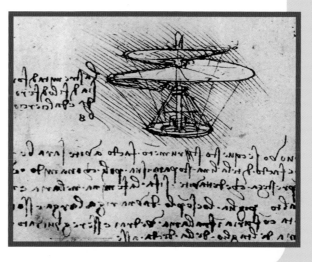

Timeline of Leonardo da Vinci

1452 Leonardo is born in Vinci, Italy.

1468 Leonardo is apprenticed to Andrea del Verrochio.

1482 Leonardo moves to Milan to work for Sforza.

1499 Leonardo goes to Florence.

1502 Leonardo works for Cesare Borgia.

1506 Leonardo returns to Milan to work for Louis XII.

1513 Leonardo moves to Rome.

1516 Leonardo goes to Amboise, France.

1519 Leonardo dies in Amboise.

⬅ A design for a helicopter. Leonardo tried to keep his work secret by using a kind of mirror-writing.

1497 Leonardo da Vinci paints *The Last Supper*.

1499 Portuguese navigator Vasco da Gama completes the first sea voyage by a European around Africa to India.

1496   1498   1500

1498 Former ruler of Florence Girolamo Savonarola is burned at the stake for heresy.

1499 A new French ruler, Louis XII, begins a more ambitious invasion of Italy.

The Study of Nature

Leonardo's sketches reflected the Renaissance belief in careful observation of the real world. In the past, artists had painted things as they "knew" they were. Now, they began to try to paint them as they really appeared. Leonardo's notebooks are full of highly detailed studies of human anatomy, clouds, waves, flowers, and other natural subjects.

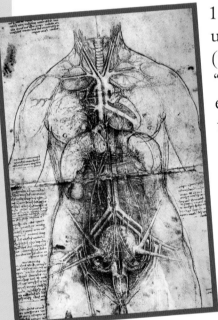

→ Leonardo made careful dissections of corpses to learn about human anatomy.

(c.1476–1507). During the years 1503–06, he painted *La Gioconda*, more commonly known as the *Mona Lisa*.

French king Louis XII (reigned 1498–1515) became his employer when he returned to Milan in 1506. After three years in Rome beginning in 1513, he went to Amboise, France, under the patronage of Francis I (reigned 1515–47), with the title of "first painter, architect, and engineer to the king." He lived there for the rest of his days.

Inventions and Designs

Throughout his life, Leonardo made sketches and plans of an amazing range of fortifications, engineering schemes, and mechanisms. He described pulleys and belt drives to transmit power,

TIMELINE
1500–1510

1500 The Treaty of Granada divides Italy between France and Spain.

1503 Czar Ivan III of Russia invades Poland-Lithuania.

c.1505 German clockmaker Peter Henlein makes a clock using springs, rather than weights; the invention enables the development of the wristwatch.

1500

1502

1504

KEY:

EUROPE

AMERICAS

AFRICA, ASIA

1500 The Portuguese explorer Pedro Álvarez Cabral claims Brazil for Portugal.

1503 Julius III becomes pope; he will be a famous patron of artists, including Michelangelo.

1505 The first African slaves arrive in the Americas at Santo Domingo.

↑ Leonardo's *The Last Supper* shows Jesus telling his disciples that one of them will betray him to the Romans.

a paddlewheel boat, and a machine for grinding glass lenses. He invented instruments for measuring the speed of a ship and the force of the wind. From watching birds in flight, he designed a man-powered, heavier-than-air flying machine with flapping wings. (It could never work because a human being could not produce enough power.) His 1485 drawing of a pyramid-shaped parachute was more practical, and he is even thought to have made some small model parachutes and tested them.

Although he was an exceptional practical engineer, Leonardo did not understand mechanics in any theoretical way. Many of his views on science differed little from the teachings of Greek scientist and philosopher Aristotle (384 B.C.–322 B.C.) 18 centuries earlier. Nevertheless, his wide-ranging talents spanning the arts and sciences made him the true Renaissance man.

Taking Notes

Leonardo made careful drawings as part of preparations for painting images. Today his notebooks are a key source of information about the artist. When Leonardo died in 1519, his friend and fellow painter Francesco Melzi carefully gathered up his paintings, papers, and models made in wood and metal. However, after Melzi's death, many were lost or destroyed. Today only about 7,000 of the original 13,000 pages of notes have survived—more than enough to testify to Leonardo's genius.

1507 The name "America" is first used in print in a German atlas.

1509 Henry VIII becomes king of England and marries his first wife, Catherine of Aragon.

1506

1508

1510

1506 Leonardo da Vinci paints the *Mona Lisa*.

1508 The League of Cambrai is formed, ranging Aragon, France, Spain, and the Holy Roman Empire against Venice.

1509 A devastating earthquake kills 10,000 people in the Ottoman capital, Istanbul.

Copernicus and the Universe

"Finally we shall place the sun himself at the center of the universe," wrote Nicolaus Copernicus. His theory changed how humans saw their place in the universe.

This statue of Copernicus holds a model solar system with the sun in the center. ⇒

TIMELINE 1510–1520

KEY:

EUROPE

ASIA

AMERICAS

1512 At the Battle of Ravenna, the French defeat the Holy League, an alliance formed by the pope to drive the French from Italy.

1513 The Union of Kalmar, which has linked Denmark, Sweden, and Norway since 1397, breaks apart as Sweden leaves.

1513 The explorer Juan Ponce de León claims Florida for Spain.

1510   1512   1514

1510 Shah Esmail I makes the Shiite branch of Islam the state religion of Persia.

1513 The Italian writer Niccolò Machiavelli writes *The Prince*, a key work that tells rulers how to exercise power.

1514 After a victory over the Persians at the Battle of Chaldiran, the Ottoman Empire expands to the east.

← These pages come
from Copernicus's work
*De Revolutionibus Orbium
Coelesteum*

Timeline of Copernicus

3rd century B.C. Aristarchus of Samos proposes the sun-centered universe.

1506 Copernicus begins work on *De Revolutionibus.*

1514 Copernicus publishes his *Little Commentary.*

1539 Rheticus publishes *Narratio Prima,* previewing Copernicus's work.

1543 *De Revolutionibus* is published.

Born in Poland on February 19, 1473, Nicolaus Copernicus studied in Krakow and in Bologna, Italy. He then became a cathedral canon in Germany. Although he later studied medicine, astronomy remained his passion.

At the time, astronomy was based on the beliefs of ancient astronomers such as Ptolemy that Earth was the center of the universe and that the sun, moon, and planets revolved around it. Ptolemy believed the heavens were perfect, so the orbits of the celestial bodies must be circular; in fact, planetary orbits are elliptical or oval. This caused many inconsistencies in Ptolemy's system.

A Sun-Centered Universe

Copernicus saw that many of the problems of Ptolemy's system would disappear if Earth moved around the sun rather than the other

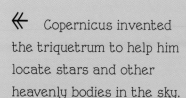

← Copernicus invented
the triquetrum to help him
locate stars and other
heavenly bodies in the sky.

1517 German monk Martin Luther begins the Reformation when he nails his Ninety-five Theses to a church door in Germany protesting the practices of the Catholic Church.

1518 Spanish authorities grant a licence allowing 4,000 African slaves to be imported to the New World.

1516

1518

1520

1516 In Venice, the Jews are made to live in a separate, walled area of the city—the world's first ghetto.

1518 Ulrich Zwingli promotes the Reformation in Zurich, Switzerland.

1519 Charles I of Spain becomes Holy Roman Emperor, linking Spain, its American colonies, Germany, and Burgundy in a single empire.

Whose Idea?

The idea that Earth and the planets orbit the sun was not new. An ancient Greek astronomer had suggested it. And in 1425, the German cleric Nicholas of Cusa suggested not only that Earth orbited the sun, but also that space was infinite and stars were other suns orbited by planets. Had Cusa's theories been more widely known, Copernicus might have found it easier to publish his more-detailed ideas during his lifetime.

way around. In 1514, he began giving out copies of a handwritten book. The book laid out the principles of the heliocentric, or sun-centered, universe: that the center of the universe was not Earth, but a point near the sun; that the universe was unimaginably large; and that the apparent movements of the sun and stars are

This image shows the sun inside the orbits of the four planets known to Copernicus. ⇒

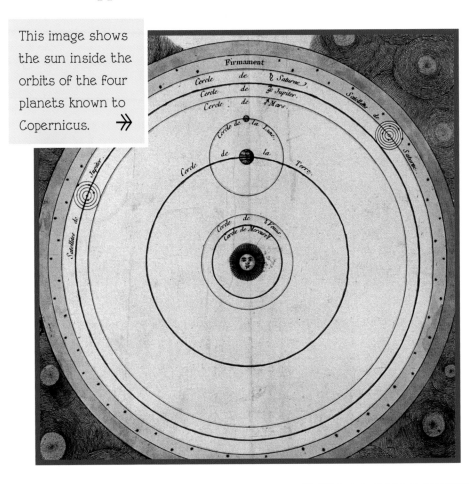

TIMELINE
1520–1530

1520 Charles V is crowned Holy Roman Emperor.

1521 War breaks out in Italy between the French, based in Milan, and the forces of Charles V and the pope.

1522 A ship from the fleet of Ferdinand Magellan completes the first circumnavigation of the world.

1520

1522

1524

KEY:

EUROPE

ASIA

AMERICAS

1520 Martin Luther is excommunicated and declared a heretic.

1521 Conquistadors led by Hernán Cortés overthrow the Aztec Empire.

1525 At the Battle of Pavia, French forces in Italy are defeated and the French king is taken captive.

↑ Today astronomers know of eight planets, their moons, and several dwarf planets circling the sun—and there may be even more.

caused by Earth's rotation on its axis and movement around the sun. The book became known as the *Little Commentary*; Copernicus saved the details for what he called his "larger work."

The Larger Work

Copernicus probably began writing *De Revolutionibus Orbium Coelestium* (On the Revolutions of the Heavenly Orbs) in 1506; he did not complete it until 1530. Because the book contradicted church teaching, he only allowed a few scientists to read the manuscript.

It was Copernicus's student, the German astronomer Rheticus (1514–1574) who persuaded him to publish *De Revolutionibus*. Rheticus published a summary in advance of publication and also oversaw the printing of the book in Nurnberg—but by the time it finally appeared, Copernicus was on his deathbed.

The First Edition

The printer of *De Revolutionibus*, Andreas Osiander, was uneasy about the idea of a sun-centered universe. He replaced Copernicus's original preface to the book with one of his own. He stated that, in truth, Earth is stationary and that the assumption that it moved around the sun was purely a device to make the calculations in the book simpler. Rheticus, not surprisingly, was furious about the new introduction—Copernicus himself probably died before he could read it.

1525 Sigismund I of Poland ends the rule of the Teutonic Knights in Prussia.

1529 Led by Sultan Suleiman the Magnificent, Ottoman forces beseige Vienna but fail to capture the city.

1526   1528   1530

1525 In Germany, the Catholic League is begun to resist the Reformation.

1527 Sweden adopts Lutheranism and cuts its ties with the papacy.

1529 By the Treaty of Saragossa, Emperor Charles V and the Portuguese divide their spheres of interest in east Asia.

The Reformation

Martin Luther saw the Catholic Church as corrupt. His efforts to reform it split the Christian faith and began a century and a half of warfare and persecution.

Martin Luther burns documents issued by the Roman Catholic Church. ⇒

TIMELINE
1530–1540

KEY:

EUROPE

ASIA

AMERICAS

1532 Conquistadors led by Francisco Pizarro conquer Peru and overthrow the Inca Empire.

1533 Henry VIII of England divorces his first wife, Catherine of Aragon, leaving him free to marry Anne Boleyn. As a result, he is excommunicated by the pope.

1535 Henry VIII assumes the title of supreme governor of the Church of England.

1530   1532   1534

1531 German Protestant princes form the Schmalkaldic League to resist the attempts of Charles V to reintroduce Catholicism.

1532 The French monk François Rabelais publishes his two great masterpieces, *Pantagruel* and *Gargantua*.

1535 A Protestant sect, the Anabaptists, seize control of Munster in Germany.

There was no shortage of reformers of the Catholic Church in the medieval period. But the crisis that began when the German monk Martin Luther nailed his Ninety-five Theses to the door of Wittenberg Castle Church in 1517 marked a change of scale. Nailing a document to a door was a common way to begin a debate at the time.

Luther's 95 points criticized what he saw as church abuses. Outraged at the sale of indulgences—documents sold for cash to buy the forgiveness of sins—Luther had become infuriated; he now accused the church of being more concerned with earthly wealth and power than heavenly salvation.

↑ To punish his criticisms, Luther was banned from church by the pope.

↠ A local prince protected Luther from the pope's forces in his castle.

Timeline of the Reformation

1517 Martin Luther nails his Ninety-five Theses to the door of Wittenberg Castle Church, Germany.

1525 William Tyndale produces an English translation of the Greek New Testament.

1529 Henry VIII clashes with the pope about a divorce from Catherine of Aragon.

1533 Henry VIII marries Anne Boleyn; he is excommunicated (expelled from the Catholic Church).

1536 William Tyndale, who has translated the Bible into English, is burned at the stake for heresy.

1539 The most famous Islamic architect, Sinan, takes charge of the Ottoman Corps of Royal Architects.

1536   1538   1540

1537 Cosimo I de Medici, a great patron of the arts, becomes duke of Florence.

1539 Agnolo Bronzino, a leading painter in the Mannerist style, becomes court artist to Cosimo de Medici.

Timeline (continued)

1534 Henry VIII breaks with Rome, creating the Church of England.

1534 Luther completes his German translation of the Bible.

1540 The Society of Jesus receives official recognition from Pope Paul III.

1541 Calvin is appointed chief pastor in Geneva.

1545 Catholic prelates meet to discuss reform at the Council of Trent in northern Italy.

1549 The Protestant *Book of Common Prayer* is published for use in all English churches.

1553 Mary I becomes queen of England, which reverts to Catholicism; Protestants are tortured and killed.

↑ John Calvin made Geneva in Switzerland a center of the Reformation.

Luther is generally considered to have been the first "Protestant." The name soon became applied to a whole range of various groups and individuals who followed his lead and eventually broke with the Catholic Church. The Protestant movement was never completely unified, however; soon Luther's own branch of Christianity—Lutheranism—was just one among many.

TIMELINE
1540–1550

1541 Protestant pastor John Calvin begins preaching in Geneva, Switzerland.

1543 Hungary is conquered by the Ottoman Turks.

1543 Andreas Vesalius publishes *On the Structure of the Human Body*, founding the modern study of human anatomy.

1540   1542   1544

KEY:

EUROPE

ASIA

AMERICAS

1540 Pope Paul III officially recognizes the Society of Jesus (the Jesuit order).

1542 War breaks out between England and France; it lasts four years.

1543 Polish astronomer Nicolaus Copernicus publishes his theory that the planets orbit the sun.

In 1520, the pope issued a decree that condemned Luther as a heretic.

The Protestants

Luther's belief that the church only interfered between individuals and their God struck a chord throughout Germany and much of northern Europe. The spirit of revolt spread rapidly, and the attack that Luther had launched on the pope's authority quickly broadened into a split.

Many protestors who took up the cause of reform were sincere believers like Luther himself. Others were more opportunistic. King Henry VIII of England first denounced Luther's views, but changed his mind when the pope refused to grant him a divorce from his marriage. The Church of England that he created was at first Catholic in everything but obedience to Rome, which Henry renounced.

John Calvin preached a very strict form of Protestantism.

1554 Mary I marries the future King Philip II of Spain, a leading Catholic power.

1555 The Peace of Augsburg allows princes in the Holy Roman Empire to decide whether their territories will be Catholic or Lutheran.

1558 Mary I is succeeded by the Protestant Elizabeth I.

1559 A first national synod (or council) of Huguenots (French Protestants) is held.

1572 The St. Bartholomew's Day Massacre takes place in Paris; hundreds of Huguenots are murdered on the orders of King Charles IX's mother, Catherine de Medici.

1545 The Council of Trent begins in Italy; it will launch the Catholic Church's Counter-Reformation.

1547 The Ottoman sultan Suleiman the Magnificent and Ferdinand of Austria sign a peace treaty.

1549 War breaks out again between England and France.

1546   1548   1550

1546 The English capture the port of Bolougne to end the Anglo-French War.

1547 Ivan I "the Terrible" becomes the first czar of Russia.

1547 The Schmalkaldic League is defeated by Hapsburg forces in the Netherlands.

The Good Book

Before the Reformation, most Bibles were in Latin, Greek, or Hebrew, which only priests could usually understand. Reformers produced the Bible in their own languages. Luther's German translation (below) appeared in 1534. The church resisted such efforts. William Tyndale, the English translator, was exiled and later burned at the stake.

New Kinds of Protestantism

Luther's own objections were to the institutions of the church and the conduct of its clergy; his faith in its central teachings still remained. In Geneva, Switzerland, however, the French preacher John Calvin rethought Christian theology altogether. He promoted a theological system that was severe and strongly Bible based. In his view, the faithful, or "elect," would be saved, but sinners would be cast into hell forever. Calvin

Protestantism was at first mostly confined to northern Europe; the south remained loyal to the pope. ⇓

majority faith 1550

- Anglican
- Catholic
- Calvinist
- Lutheran
- Muslim
- Orthodox
- mixed

TIMELINE
1550–1560

1552 The Russians begin an expansion by conquering the former Mongol khanate of Kazan.

1555 By the Peace of Augsburg, Charles V agrees to allow local rulers in Germany to decide the official religion in their territories.

1550   1552   1554

KEY:

EUROPE

ASIA

AMERICAS

1550 The French recapture Bolougne from the English.

1553 Under Mary I, Catholicism is restored as the official religion in England; hundreds of Protestants are killed.

The gospell of S. Mathew.
The fyrst Chapter.

← William Tyndale's English translation of the Bible appeared in 1525.

even argued that God already knew which group was which and that some people were thus destined to be damned. In English-speaking countries, Calvin's followers became known as Puritans. They were famous for their strict morality and their often intolerant attitude to those who did not share their beliefs.

Political Effects

The political effect of the Reformation was to split first Europe and later other parts of the world into opposing Protestant and Catholic camps. Protestants were persecuted in Catholic lands, Catholics in the growing number of Protestant ones, but many braved torture and death rather than surrender their beliefs.

The Counter-Reformation

Thoughtful Catholics soon came to realize that there was some justice in Luther's complaints. Loyal to the pope, they tried to combat the Protestants by cleansing the church of abuses from within. Leading churchmen met at the Council of Trent (1545–63) to draft the reforms. Meanwhile, a group of dedicated Catholic writers, artists, and priests mobilized to reinvigorate the faith in the intellectual and spiritual movement called the Counter-Reformation.

1556 In England, the Archbishop of Canterbury, Thomas Cranmer, is burned at the stake for his Protestant beliefs.

1559 The Treaty of Cateau-Cambrésis ends two long-running European conflicts: between France and the Hapsburgs, when France gives up all claims in Italy; and between France and the English, who give up Calais, their last territory in France.

1556   1558   1560

1556 Charles V gives up his throne. His son Philip II inherits Spain, the Netherlands, Naples, and Milan; Charles's brother Ferdinand becomes Holy Roman Emperor and takes the territory in central Europe.

1558 Elizabeth I becomes queen of England on the death of Mary I.

Ivan the Terrible

Ivan Vasilyevich was the first Russian ruler to use the title "czar." His harsh, cruel reign did much to shape the destiny of Russia and create its character.

St. Basil's Cathedral in Moscow was built to celebrate Ivan's military victories. →→

TIMELINE
1560–1570

1561 Charles IX becomes king of France at age 13; real power lies in the hands of his mother, Catherine de Medici.

1562 Saint Teresa of Avila founds the new order of Discalced Carmelite nuns.

1563 Philip II begins to build the Escorial, a palace-monastery, outside Madrid in Spain.

1560   1562   1564

1561 In India, Akbar the Great takes the throne of the Mughal Empire, which will experience a golden age under his rule.

1562 Huguenots (Protestants) revolt in southern France.

1565 The Mediterranean island of Malta resists a four-month siege by the Ottomans.

KEY:

EUROPE

ASIA

AFRICA

Born in 1533, Ivan Vasilyevich became grand duke of Muscovy at age three. Only five years later, his mother and regent died; her orphaned son was manipulated by the different factions of *boyars* (nobles) at the Moscow court. But Ivan had his own ideas and, at 13, ordered his first assassination. In 1547, he took power, becoming the first Russian ruler to use the title "czar" (from the Roman "Caesar"). His marriage to Anastasia Zakharina soon after seems to have stabilized his life to some extent.

Ivan's Reign

Ivan's reign began well. The young ruler showed a skill for effective action when in 1552 he conquered the Mongol khanate of Kazan. The next year he reopened trade with

↑ A worker displays a religious icon of Ivan's father, Vasily III.

Timeline of Ivan the Terrible

1533 Ivan Vasilyevich is born.

1536 Ivan's father, Vasily III, dies: Ivan becomes grand duke of Muscovy (Moscow) with his mother as regent.

1538 Ivan's mother is murdered.

1547 Ivan takes personal power, the first Russian ruler to bear the title "czar."

1552 Ivan's forces conquer the Mongol khanate of Kazan.

1553 The English explorer Richard Chancellor opens up the trade route around the North Cape of Norway to Russia's White Sea.

1553 Ivan's infant son Dmitri drowns in a tragic accident.

⇐ The "terrible" in Ivan's name is in fact more accurately translated as "awesome."

1567 Scotland's Catholic ruler Mary, Queen of Scots, is removed by a confederacy of Protestant nobles.

1569 The Union of Lublin unites Poland and Lithuania; the enlarged nation comes into conflict with Russia.

1566

1568

1570

1567 Philip II sends the Duke of Alba to stop protests in the Spanish Netherlands, but his harsh measures start a full revolt.

1569 Moriscos, Spanish Muslims who have nominally converted to Christianity, rebel against Philip II.

Timeline (continued)

1555 Construction of St. Basil's Cathedral, Moscow, begins.

1556 Ivan's forces conquer Astrakhan.

1558 Eager to gain access to the Baltic Sea, Ivan launches the first of a series of wars against Livonia that will stretch on for 25 years.

1560 Ivan's wife Anastasia dies.

1569 The Union of Lublin unites Lithuania with Poland.

1570 Ivan punishes the "Novgorod Treason" with a reign of terror in the city.

1581 The czar murders his second son, Ivan.

1584 Death of Ivan the Terrible. He is succeeded by his third son, Fyodor.

the West. He extended his kingdom again in 1556, taking the khanate of Astrakhan and opening the way to the Volga River, the Caspian Sea, the Caucasus Mountains, and Siberia. In 1558, he attacked the Livonian Knights, who restricted Russian access to the Baltic Sea. The

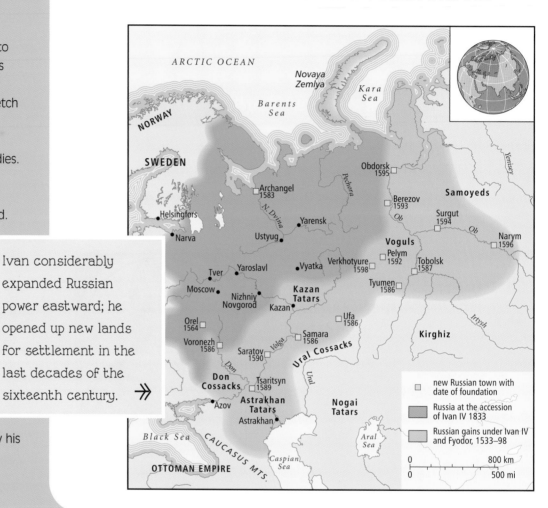

Ivan considerably expanded Russian power eastward; he opened up new lands for settlement in the last decades of the sixteenth century. →

TIMELINE 1570–1580

KEY:

EUROPE

ASIA

AFRICA

1572 The Dutch War of Independence against the Spanish governor of the Netherlands, the Duke of Alba, gathers pace.

1572 The Portuguese poet Luis de Camoes publishes the national epic, *The Lusiads*.

1570   1572   1574

1571 A Christian fleet defeats a large Ottoman fleet at the Battle of Lepanto, off the coast of Greece.

1572 More than 2,500 leading Huguenots are killed in Paris in the Massacre of Saint Bartholomew's Day.

1575 The Greek painter Domenikos Theotokopolous settles in Toledo, Spain, where he achieves fame as El Greco, "the Greek."

← In his later reign, Ivan became more unpredictable and cruel in his behavior.

campaign turned into a long war with Sweden.

Decline and Death

After Anastasia's death in 1560, Ivan grew paranoid. He split his kingdom into two, the *oprichnina* or area around Moscow, which was under his own control, and the *zemshchina*, which was run by a boyars' council. In practice, Ivan's own 6,000-strong secret police force, the black-hooded *oprichniki*, roamed the *zemshchina* at will, terrorizing the population and pulling in suspects for torture sessions in which Ivan himself sometimes took part. No one was safe: The head of the Russian Orthodox Church was one victim of the terror; another was Ivan's cousin, Prince Vladimir Staritsky. In 1581, in a rage, the czar even murdered his own son, Ivan. He himself died in 1584. He left Russia comparatively strong and coherent as a nation, but economically backward and ruled by fear.

St. Basil's

St. Basil's Cathedral in Moscow (below) is one of the world's most famous buildings. It was built as a monument to the conquests of Ivan I. In fact, the czar's relations with the Orthodox Church were strained. He did not like the hold the church had over Russia's peasants, but he needed it to back his authority with the people.

1576 Rudolf II of Hungary becomes Holy Roman Emperor; his court in Prague becomes a center for writers, artists, and scholars.

1577 Death of Titian, the greatest painter of the late Renaissance.

1576

1578

1580

1576 In response to the Dutch revolt, Spanish troops sack Antwerp in the Netherlands, killing 7,000 citizens.

1579 The seven rebel provinces of the Netherlands form the Union of Utrecht under the leadership of William the Silent.

Elizabeth's England

Later generations looked back on the reign of Elizabeth I as a golden age. England changed from a country divided by strife to one of peace, stability, and prosperity.

Queen Elizabeth controlled her public image as carefully as any modern politician. →→

TIMELINE
1580–1590

1582 The Mughal emperor Akbar sets out his Divine Faith, which incorporates elements of many religions.

1582 Pope Gregory XIII introduces the Gregorian calendar to replace the Julian calendar.

1584 The Russians open the port of Archangel on the White Sea, giving them limited access to the ocean.

1580   1582   1584

KEY:

EUROPE

1580 Philip II of Spain claims the throne of Portugal.

ASIA

1584 On the death of Ivan IV, the noble Boris Godunov becomes virtual ruler of Russia in place of Ivan's simple son Fyodor.

AMERICAS

← Mary Tudor tried to return England to the Catholic faith.

Born in 1533, Elizabeth was the daughter of King Henry VIII and his second wife, Anne Boleyn. In order to divorce his first wife, Catherine of Aragon, Henry split with the Roman Catholic Church and declared himself head of the new Church of England. But Anne failed to produce the son Henry wanted; less than three years after Elizabeth's birth, she was executed on the king's orders. Meanwhile, the young princess had the education usually reserved for the male heirs of Renaissance monarchs and was instructed in Greek, Latin, history, philosophy, and theology as well as French and Italian.

Brief Reigns

Henry died in 1547 and was succeeded by Edward VI, the 10-year-old son of his third wife, Jane Seymour. When Edward died suddenly at age 16, his eldest

Timeline of Elizabeth's England

1533 Elizabeth is born at Greenwich Palace, London.

1536 Elizabeth's mother, Anne Boleyn, is executed.

1554 Queen Mary suspects Elizabeth of treason and holds her prisoner.

1558 On the death of Mary, Elizabeth is crowned queen of England.

1559 Elizabeth becomes supreme governor of the Church of England.

1585 Elizabeth sends an army to the Netherlands to support a revolt against Spain.

1587 Mary, queen of Scots, Elizabeth's cousin, is found guilty of plotting against the queen and executed.

← The Spanish armada (fleet) tried unsuccessfully to invade England in 1588.

1588 Abbas I becomes shah of Persia; he will be the greatest of the Safavid rulers and a great patron of the arts.

1586   1588   1590

1585 Queen Elizabeth I receives a diplomatic letter from the Sultan of Aceh in Indonesia.

1589 Henry of Navarre, a Protestant, becomes the first of the Bourbon kings of France as Henry IV.

1589 Philip II of Spain declares war on France in support of Catholics opposed to Henry IV.

Timeline (continued)

1588 The Spanish Armada, with 130 warships, tries to invade England.

1590 Edmund Spenser publishes the first three books of *The Faerie Queene*, a narrative poem written in celebration of Elizabeth.

1598 The Globe Theater opens in London with a performance of William Shakespeare's play *Henry V*.

1601 Robert Devereux, earl of Essex, Elizabeth's former favorite, leads a rebellion against her; he is executed for treason.

1603 Elizabeth dies and is succeeded by James VI of Scotland, son of Mary, queen of Scots.

Elizabethan England

English settlement in Ireland to 1603

route of the Spanish Armada 1588

battle between the English and Spanish fleets

ATLANTIC OCEAN

Orkney Islands

Outer Hebrides

Inverness

Aberdeen

SCOTLAND

Dundee

Inner Hebrides

Stirling

Glasgow

Edinburgh

Berwick upon Tweed

North Sea

L. Neagh

Belfast

Carlisle

Newcastle

Sligo

Dundalk

IRELAND

Drogheda

Isle of Man

York

Kingston upon Hull

Galway

Dublin

Irish Sea

Liverpool

Anglesey

Caernarvon

Nottingham

Trent

Norwich

Limerick

Severn

Birmingham

Cambridge

Tralee

Waterford

Wexford

Northampton

Ipswich

Cork

Tenby

Gloucester

ENGLAND

Oxford

Thames

London

Bristol

Canterbury

Celtic Sea

Southampton

Calais

Exeter

Portsmouth

Plymouth

English Channel

FRANCE

Dieppe

Cherbourg

Rouen

remnants of Armada return to Spain

0   200 km
0   150 mi

↑ After fighting battles in the English Channel, the Armada was swept north by storms to Scotland.

Sir Francis Drake became a British hero for his role in defeating the Armada. ⇒

half-sister, Mary, the Catholic daughter of Catherine of Aragon, became queen. Mary had many Protestants killed. These were unhappy years for Elizabeth. By

TIMELINE
1590–1600

1590 The Ottoman and Safavid empires make peace and fix their frontier at the Caspian Sea.

1593 Henry IV ends the French Wars of Religion by giving up his Protestant faith and being accepted by his Catholic subjects.

1594 Hugh O'Neill, earl of Tyrone, leads an Irish rebellion against English rule.

1590   1592   1594

KEY:

EUROPE

ASIA

AMERICAS

1590 John Hartington, a courtier of Queen Elizabeth, invents the flush toilet.

c.1595 The telescope is invented in the Netherlands.

the time she found herself queen on the death of Mary in 1558, she was already well skilled in the arts of political survival.

Elizabeth's Reign

From the beginning, Elizabeth ruled strongly, kept her own counsel, chose her advisers carefully, and maintained good relations with Parliament. One of her first moves was to restore Protestantism in England, but she rejected the extreme measures employed by both Edward and Mary to enforce religious change. She believed that England needed a period of stability and calm to recover from the religious and political upheavals of the recent past.

Elizabeth never married but instead built up a strong personal cult, surrounding herself with courtiers, poets, and painters who celebrated her image as the Virgin Queen. Her reign was a time of expansion for England: Sir Francis Drake, Sir John Hawkins, and Sir Walter Raleigh, among other adventurers, helped make the country rich through exploration, trade, and plunder. Their exploits overseas, especially against the power of Spain, added to the newfound sense of national pride that Elizabeth's long reign helped forge.

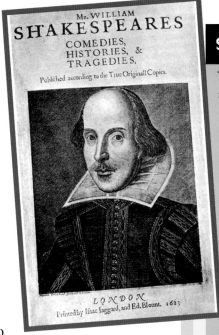

Mr. WILLIAM SHAKESPEARES COMEDIES, HISTORIES, & TRAGEDIES. Published according to the True Originall Copies. LONDON Printed by Isaac Iaggard, and Ed. Blount. 1623

Shakespeare

William Shakespeare, the greatest writer of the Elizabethan age, was born in 1564 in the town of Stratford-upon-Avon. By the early 1590s, he was living in London, where he joined the Lord Chamberlain's Men, a company of actors paid for by the royal purse. Shakespeare soon found fame as the author of plays that won him popular acclaim and favor at court. His words, phrases, and characters have entered the English language and imagination. He died in Stratford in 1616.

1596 The Spanish crown is bankrupt; famine and plague reduce the population over the coming years.

1598 The Treaty of Vervins ends the Spanish war with France.

1598 Boris Gudunov is elected czar of Russia.

1596   1598   1600

1595 Francis Drake, an English buccaneer, attacks Panama, the heart of Spain's overseas empire.

1597 Shah Abbas of Persia moves the capital to Esfahan.

1598 Henry IV signs the Edict of Nantes, which guarantees religious freedom in France.

Glossary

armada The Spanish word for a military fleet. Specifically, it refers to a fleet of 130 ships sent by Spain to invade England in 1588.

arquebus An early type of portable gun supported on a tripod or forked rest and braced against the shoulder. Sometimes spelled "harquebus."

astrolabe An instrument used by sailors to measure the position of the sun to help estimate their position at sea.

caravel A small sailing ship that was strong enough to withstand ocean winds and currents.

czar The title of the ruler of Russia, derived from the Roman title "caesar."

excommunication A judgment issued by the pope or a bishop banning an individual from participating in the rites of the Catholic Church for a limited or indefinite period.

fresco A method of painting directly onto wet plaster.

heretic A person who rejects the official version of religion.

humanism A worldview popularized during the Renaissance that made human beings rather than God the focus of intellectual attention.

incunabulum Any book printed in Europe before 1501 (plural: incunabula).

indulgence A paper sold by the Catholic Church to grant forgiveness for sins, thereby shortening the time a sinner would spend in Purgatory after his or her death.

movable type In printing, small rectangular blocks each bearing a raised letter or other character.

New World A name first used in the sixteenth-century to describe the Western Hemisphere, especially the continents of North and South America. The name distinguished newly discovered lands from the "Old World" of Europe and Asia.

papacy The ruling body of the Catholic Church, headed by the pope.

Protestant A word describing any of the churches or their members that broke from the Roman Catholic Church in the course of the Reformation.

Further Reading

Books
Arnold, David. *Age of Discovery, 1400–1600.* New York: Routledge, 2002.

Brotton, Jerry. *The Renaissance: A Very Short Introduction.* New York: Oxford University Press, 2006.

Cole, Alison. *Eyewitness: Renaissance.* New York: DK Children, 2000.

Collinson, Patrick. *The Reformation: A History.* New York: Modern Library, 2006.

Crompton, Samuel Willard. *Queen Elizabeth and England's Golden Age.* Philadelphia: Chelsea House Publications, 2005.

Edwards, Roberta. *Who Was Leonardo da Vinci?* New York: Grosset & Dunlap, 2005.

MacCulloch, Diarmaid. *The Reformation.* New York: Penguin, 2005.

Madariaga, Isabel de. *Ivan the Terrible.* New Haven: Yale University Press, 2006.

Payne, Robert. *Ivan the Terrible.* New York: Cooper Square Press, 2002.

Plumb, J. H. *The Italian Renaissance.* Boston: Mariner Books, 2001.

Rabb, Theodore. *Renaissance Lives: Portraits of an Age.* New York: Basic Books, 2001.

Repcheck, Jack. *Copernicus' Secret: How the Scientific Revolution Began.* New York: Simon & Schuster, 2008.

Shuter, Jane. *The Renaissance.* Chicago: Heinemann-Raintree, 2007.

Slater, John Rothwell. *Printing and the Renaissance.* New York: Dodo Press, 2008.

Web Sites
www.teacheroz.com/ renaissance.htm
List of sites and timelines

history-world.org/ renaissance.htm
Detailed history of the Renaissance with an emphasis on art

www.kidspast.com/world-history/0288-the-renaissance.php
Introduction to the Renaissance period

www.socialstudiesforkids.com/ subjects/renaissance.htm
Links to art and history web sites

Index

age of discovery 10–15
    international trade
        and 11–13
    routes taken 12
arquebus 18, **18**
astrolabe **11**
Calvin, John **35**, 36–37
cannon **16**, 17, **17**, **18**, 19
    metal casting and 19
Cape of Good Hope **11**
caravel 14, **14**
Columbus, Christopher
    13–14, 15, **15**
compass **15**
Copernicus, Nicolaus
    28–31, **28**
    and the Catholic
        Church 31
    and the sun-centered
        universe 29–30, **30**
da Vinci, Leonardo 23,
    24–27, **25**
    and the natural sciences
        26, **26**
    inventions and designs
        25, 26–27
    notebooks 27
De Revolutionibus
    Orbium Coelestium 31
Dias, Bartholemeu 13
Drake, Francis **44**
early printed books 9
Elizabeth I of England
    42, 42–45
    cult of personality
        and 45

See also Shakespeare,
    Spanish Armada
Erasmus, Desiderius
    23, **23**
Florence Cathedral **21**
Gama, Vasco de **12**, 13
guns and gunpowder
    16–19
    origins 17
    use in warfare 18–19
    See also cannon,
        arquebus
Gutenberg, Johannes
    7, **7**, 8, 9
Henry the Navigator 13,
    13, 14
illuminated letters **6**
incunabula. *See* early
    printed books
Ivan the Terrible 38–41,
    39, **41**
    conquests 39–41, **40**
    mental decline and
        death 41
Last Supper, The (da Vinci)
    25, **26–27**
Luther, Martin **32**, 32–36,
    33, **35**
Marco Polo 14
Michaelangelo **20**
movable type 8–9, **9**
    See also printing
Nicholas of Cusa 30
Nuremberg Chronicle **8**
printing 6–9
    in ancient China 7, 8

presses 8–9, **9**
    See also Gutenberg,
        Johannes
Reformation, the 32–37
    Catholic response 37
    Henry VIII of England
        and 35
    political effects 37
    sale of indulgences
        and 33
    translating the Bible
        and 36, **37**
    See also Luther, Martin
Renaissance 20–23
    Byzantine Empire and
        21
    city design and **22**
    humanism and 23
Rheticus 31
Schwarz, Berthold **19**, 19
Shakespeare 45, **45**
Sistine Chapel **20**
Spanish Armada **43**, **44**
St. Basil's Cathedral,
    Moscow **38**, 41, **41**
triquetium **29**
Vasily III of Russia **39**